The
Little Lamb

A Random House PICTUREBACK®

The Little Lamb

Story by Judy Dunn

Photographs by Phoebe Dunn

Random House 🏠 New York

Library of Congress Cataloging in Publication Data: Dunn, Judy. The little lamb. SUMMARY: A young girl adopts a lamb in early spring and raises him until he is big enough to return to the flock. 1. Lambs—Juvenile literature. [1. Sheep] I. Dunn, Phoebe. II. Title. SF375.2.D86 1978 636.3'07 76-24167 ISBN:0-394-83440-2 (B.C.), 0-394-83455-0 (trade); 0-394-93455-5 (lib. bdg.).

One afternoon in early spring,
Emmy walked over to the
Wetherbee Farm. There were
twenty newborn lambs
in the flock, and Emmy
couldn't wait to see them.

All the lambs had long, wobbly legs and little pointed hoofs.
Most of them were white, but a few were black. Emmy stood
on a rock and watched them follow their mothers into the barn.

Mother sheep usually keep their babies close to them.
But one little white lamb wandered away from the flock.
He seemed to be lost. *Baa-baa-baa,* he cried.

Emmy jumped off the rock and the little lamb ran
right up to her.

Mrs. Wetherbee asked Emmy if she would like to take care of the lamb until he was big enough to come back to the flock. He had a twin brother, and their mother did not have enough milk for two babies.

Emmy was so happy she bent over and kissed the little lamb. Then she gently picked him up and carried him home.

He was cuddly and warm, and she could feel his heart beating. Emmy decided to call her lamb Timothy.

That evening Emmy heated milk for her lamb. She sat down under the maple tree and gave him his bottle.

At first he wiggled and chewed the rubber nipple. Warm milk dripped all over Emmy. But Timothy quickly learned to sit still and drink his milk.

Emmy was a good mother to Timothy. She fed him
twice a day and gave him plenty of love. Soon Timothy
followed Emmy wherever she went.

By summertime the little lamb didn't need to drink milk from a bottle any more. He was big enough to eat grain out of a dish. His fleece had grown thick and woolly.

Emmy put a collar and bell around Timothy's neck. He slept in the barn, curled up in the warm straw outside the horse's stall.

On sunny summer days, Emmy
and Timothy went to the fields
together. While they played
hide-and-seek, Midnight the cat
chased after bumblebees.

Emmy would hide in the
tall grass. But sooner or later,
Timothy always found her.

When Timothy was tired,
he plopped down to rest
on Emmy's lap.

Sometimes Emmy liked to
make dandelion chains and
pretend she was a princess.
The only trouble was—
Timothy ate the dandelions.

When Emmy wasn't around to play, Timothy always seemed to get into mischief.

He would rub his back against the sheets on the clothesline, or jump into the laundry basket for a nap.

One morning Timothy tipped over a basket on the porch. *Bumpity-bumpity-bump.* A whole bushel of apples bounced down the steps.

Then Timothy scampered
into the garden. He ate
the tops off all the radishes
and trampled the lettuce
plants.

After that he started
eating the primroses.

Emmy found Timothy
hiding behind the house—
full of vegetables and
flowers and feeling
quite sick. She poured
some medicine into
a spoon and Timothy
swallowed it all.

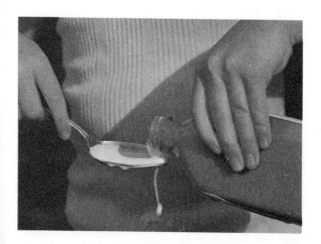

The next day Timothy was
feeling fine. Emmy decided
to give him a bath. She wanted
him to look his best because they
were going to a birthday party.

Emmy filled the washtub with
warm, soapy water and scrubbed
Timothy's ears and chin. She
shampooed his fleece until it
was soft and white.

Then she rubbed him down
with a fuzzy towel. Later on,
when he was dry, she combed
his woolly coat.

Emmy's father drove them to the party in his truck.
Emmy was wearing her party dress, and Timothy had
a new purple leash.

The birthday party was lots
of fun. All the children wore
paper hats, and bright balloons
hung over the table.

When the children sat down
for ice cream and cake, Emmy
tied her lamb to the table to
keep him close.

Suddenly...BANG...
a balloon popped!

The loud noise
frightened Timothy.
He tried to run away.

The table collapsed,
the ice cream spilled,
and the cake slid to
the ground.
What a mess!
That evening Emmy's
father said Timothy was
getting too big to keep
as a pet.

Early the next morning,
Emmy walked Timothy
to the Wetherbee Farm.
She hugged Timothy's
woolly neck and promised
to visit whenever she could.

Then she took off his purple leash and Timothy scampered out to meet the flock.

He buried his nose in a clover patch, and grazed with the other sheep in the morning sun.

Timothy was back where he belonged.
Now there were twenty lambs again
at the Wetherbee Farm.